# MAKE MONEY WITH AMAZON

## HOW TO MAKE OVER $1,000 PER DAY ON AMAZON:

## OVER 100 NICHES THAT WILL MAKE YOU A TON OF MONEY,

## SELL HOT PRODUCTS THAT WILL MAKE YOU PASSIVE INCOME,

## A BEGINNERS OR ADVANCED GUIDE

Tim Steinberg

purposes only and are the owned by the owners themselves, not affiliated with this document.

# Table of Contents

# INTRODUCTION

You are now reading the best-selling book on Amazon about "Make Money with Amazon."

We all could use more money, how about a lot of money! Each and every day you could be earning passive income while you sleep in the hundreds of thousands of dollars, No! I am not kidding.

Think about how fantastic your life could be, if your income was $200,000 or more a year. And best of all, you didn't need to clock in at a job working for someone else day after day. We all heard the saying before all work and no play makes jack a dull boy, well how about all work and no pay instead of play, because essentially when you slave away at a 9 to 5 job you are not getting really what you are worth, and that will make you cold and sad in a hurry.

These employers don't take into account how you feel, you are a number, a tool, and when you are no good anymore you are no good use to them. Life was meant to be free and to live on your own terms. That is the American dream.

Think of how fantastic it would be if you really started making six figure income regularly, more cash and all done on your own time with little to no effort. Here are some of the benefits of doing business, taking action and getting ahead in life:

- Work with little to no effort, wherever and whenever, you are the boss
- Live the dream life, buy any luxury item you want, no more wishful thinking, take that vacation you always wanted
- Never beg a boss again to take a lunch break, or ask for vacation time off

- Never worry about a 401K again, retirement who? Live your life now, rather than saving up for a time when you may not be able to enjoy it.

This book you have in your hands now will show you this method to all these things and much much more. . .

You are Fantastic!

Thank you for downloading this book!

I'm going to show you just how you can make a ton of money on Amazon whether as an affiliate or with Fulfillment by Amazon (FBA). I know there is a million more ways to make money online with Amazon, but this a true and proven method to end all your financial woes and get back into the fast lane. . .you with me? Let's get started

There are many niche products you can sell and promote as either a sole proprietor or as an affiliate.

You can even sell with what's known as am eCommerce site or directly with Amazon the choice is yours. You are always in the driver's seat.

# AMAZON BUSINESS 2.0

I will show you step by step and reveal over 100 fantastic and mid range to expensive top level products from over 15 different niches that are already making people thousands if not millions. This may seem too good to be true, thinking that the market is already saturated, but keep this in mind, Amazons search engine alone brings in millions of traffic even on the same level with Google or even passing them, in short there is room for everybody.

It doesn't matter if you are a affiliate already of Amazon you can still pick up lots of how to information that you may have not known even the ability to promote fast for passive income and huge commissions.

The choice is yours whether you are looking into Amazons FBA, eCommerce, drop shipping, or AliBaba. As you know the products listed here are good sellers. Finally we I will show you just how to hack yourself to success with these niches and products and much much more.
. .

You Ready? Let do this, let's get started with finding some hot product niches to make some big money.

## Overview

Here is what you will learn:

Over 100 Amazon products that that you can sell easily and fast as an affiliate if you choose to be or not. You will still make sales.

Strategies the pros use, to hack yourself to instant success and make income as an affiliate of Amazon.

Over 15+ Red Hot niches on Amazon you can make money from and much much more. .

**What You Will Learn in This Book**

No prior knowledge or experience is necessary, with these techniques you can:

- Learn the same step by step process I used to go from zero money to hundreds of thousands of dollars in little to no time, all using your computer, and it works time after time
- Make passive income while you sleep, the money literally flows direct deposit into your account, no extra work necessary, no more W2 forms, no more pesky background checks
- Get to the point where everything is on auto pilot, you can even hire assistants very cheaply to do meaningless tasks such as checking email, and answering messages.
- Everything can be up and running in one day, even if you are not very good at using the internet.
- Make your first earnings fast, direct deposit to your bank
- Learn the system fast and keep earning with little to no effort, avoid the traps and pitfalls
- This book will show you step by step how I went from quitting my job for good, and making over $400 dollars a day every day with no effort at all, working right from the comfort of my own home on my own time.

# MY STORY

### A little about me

My life took a turn when I quit my job, confused and down on life, I turned to surfing the net, I scoured over everything I could on how to make money fast, how to make money online, creating a app for smart phones, but all these methods wanted a lot of money to get started and nothing in return, and some were outright cheating scammers to say the least, which made me more depressed. Then I stumbled onto a technique through a secret Facebook group on how to make money the real way, all online and no experience necessary. I thought here we go again, but I said what the hell and gave it another shot. I quickly learned about living anywhere you want, work anytime and still make money using only your computer. I thought WOW! This is it. And this is how I learned all these techniques I am about to reveal to you.

I quickly went from earning $1000 on my first try to well over $200,000 in a few months, I was finding more and more clients and well, I won't spoil it for you, but if you are getting as excited as I was then, keep with me. . .

I should also tell you that this manual is a work in progress. It is complete, just as it is, in your hands. It contains all the information you could want to make money faster than you ever thought possible.

But it is a manual that is far better than the manual that was produced last year. Almost monthly, I make changes, offer improvements, and introduce new strategies and new ideas. I'm constantly trying to improve this Amazon money making success manual.

That's why it's produced in the form you see now. This manual format allows me to give you the latest version with the most up to the minute changes. You're not getting a manual that is years old, with antiquated information. You're getting the very latest thoughts. In many cases, you're reading much of what I was evolving just last week!!

No other manual can give you that kind of timeliness.
I also want you to know that the technique for making money with your computer in 1 day applies to both men and women, young and old, even if you are new to the internet. Anyone can make money at unbelievable speeds, all you need is a desktop computer or laptop, even your smart phone will do, and a good internet connection and you are good to go.

**HOW DO YOU LIKE THE BOOK SO FAR?**

Type this link in your browser to go to Amazon

bit.ly/timsteinberg

If you're undecided, just leave a review later...

# How Much Money Can I make Using These Methods

If someone came to you with a machine and told you they could turn your $5 bill into a $10 bill, and after looking at the process you discovered it was legit and you really could buy $10 for $5, there wasn't any catch--in fact, they actually guaranteed your success--what would you do?

If you were a normal, breathing, thinking, human being, you'd get as many five-dollar bills as you could find. You'd clean out your bank account, mortgage your house, and borrow from banks, friends, and strangers. You'd set up partnerships, climb mountains, cash in your securities, and sell your furniture!

Well, that machine is what you've got in your hands right now. You've got a book, a machine that will literally show you how to produce the most powerful marketing tool you or your business will ever encounter. Just days from now you'll have that marketing tool and you'll be using it to harvest more revenue, bring in more clients, rocket your own career and experience more success than you may have thought possible.

How much money you make will depend on how focused you are, how bad you want it all, there is no set limit, I went from very little money to hundreds of thousands of dollars and within months, I have clients who I coach that are making $20,000 a month, so really the amount is up to you, how much do you want to make, there is no limit. The myth is work hard and you will succeed, that is true to some degree, but not true all across the board, you have to jump to get to the top, not stay with the flock.

Make no mistake I won't ask you join money groups, fake stock market ads, sell makeup online, sell on eBay, and take surveys or bitcoins.

These business techniques are easy, fast, and efficient at bringing you cash flow and passive income with little to no effort, and best of all you don't need money to start.

# WHO NEEDS THIS BOOK

Anyone who is tired and down and out on life with their rat race job, the stay at home mom who wants that income so she can make her kids and herself happy, the struggling to meet payments worker who is already working 3 jobs, lost your job, found a new job, don't have a job, it doesn't matter these techniques don't discriminate and can work for anyone. I have used these strategies to go from nothing to making over $400 dollars a day, everyday! I can show you the way; all you need are these things:

- Do you have access to a laptop or desktop computer?
- Do you have the internet at home?
- Do you speak English?
- Are you familiar with sending email?
- Do you know how to use Microsoft Word, Excel?
- Do you know how to perform research with all the major search engines, like Google, Yahoo, and Bing?

# WHO DOESN'T NEED THIS BOOK

People who want something for nothing, lazy, unwilling to learn, procrastinators, no goals in life, not driven. If any of these apply to you simply send your book back for a full refund and I will be more than happy to issue you the refund no questions asked.

To make money you have to be willing to put in the effort, I won't ask of you to do anything out of the ordinary, but we are in this together, I am here for you every step of the way, your success makes me happy, I always had a goal to give back when I made it. Don't make the mistakes I made when first starting out trying to make it rich, I had to figure everything out all by myself, and I wasted time, but now you don't have to because I am detailing everything out, with all the clutter gone, only instant success.

# BE PERSISTENT, BE DRIVEN

I say this because what matters most in life and your success in this business model is that you have persistence and drive, its one thing to say "yah yah, I'll do it tomorrow" and it's another thing to really be confident and have the drive to push forward no matter what anyone says.

I know. I made a lot of money this way and have fully investigated all the best educational short cuts for three years.

I never quit, because quitters never make it to the top, I would never be where I am today if I didn't have the drive and determination I set out to be, by making millions. And I know you have this drive and burning desire in you as well or you would not be reading this book. Life is exploration and making the money you want is all about having fun and knowing the how-to information, it's all there, but you just have to open your eyes and take advantage of it all.

The methods I am going to teach you will allow you to do just what I did, I went from earning $400 dollars a day to well over $300,000 in as little as 6 months, all with little time and effort, it was really cool.
There are many ways to make money online, but with; drop shipping, eBay, Google ads, Facebook, and more, but these techniques I will show you will literally blow your socks off.

**Money and Profits are Coming Your Way**

My commitment to you, I will share with you everything I learned and know, I will hold nothing back for a new book, you will learn everything I did to get where I am at now, and have a full business up and running for yourself. Everything is possible, trust me.

These techniques you are going to learn in this book will show you exactly how to use your computer like a machine to make money. All I ask of you is to never give up, things will get hard, you may get frustrated, but at the end it will all pay off. .

Please try the techniques. They work over and over again. I have students all over the world who are successfully making money right from their own home with little to no effort with these techniques.

The ONLY reason you could possibly fail to make hundreds of thousands of dollars of more is that you decide not to follow the guidelines.

I look forward to seeing you make lots of money, and to hearing about your success!

# 6 REASONS WHY AMAZON IS THE MOST FANTASTIC WAY TO MAKE MONEY

"Rule number 1: Never lose money. Rule number 2: Never forget rule number 1."

Warren Buffett

Now you are really excited about making money with Amazon, I want to turn you attention to the many perks that go along with this business and how much money you can really make.

### 1. The Potential for Earnings is Incredibly High

The really neat thing about making money with Amazon is that you can earn a lot of money in a short period of time. When I started, I was making $150 dollars a day on two sales, which was nice, but I thought I

12

could do better, within a few months I was making well over $135,000 dollars and that was in one month.

There are many reasons why my earnings increased this quick.
Your earning will depend on how fast you research a particular niche and whether or not it is profitable; and how well you research your keywords. When you get good at it and you have the system down, then you become faster and money will start to flow from those sales. After a while, you will find yourself researching a profitable niche and making deals with big website owners in no time, getting the products for cheap and no hidden fees paying. Search for another niche and watch the money roll in. Instantly!
Don't worry if all these terms, such as Keywords, niche, category, sound hard, we all have to start somewhere. With a bit of time you will be learning fast how everything works and making money in no time. I will provide you with all the resources and websites and where to click and all, remember it's all step by step and easy, I got your back every step of the way. I hold nothing back as many authors and courses do. I lay it all on the table.

**Here's an example of my earnings for 2017**

(The screenshots show amounts for 2017, I omitted my account number of course.)
The point is that your potential earnings for this are high, as you move along and gain more experience you will see just how easy it is.

13

Some niches may pay only $500 a day but many will pay thousands of dollars or more.

Here's an example of one client of mine, he offered me $1000 for a particular product I was selling, then he wanted me to do some research for him on a particular niche and product, I did more work for this client, why not, they liked my work and I liked their money, and if you look at my earnings for 2017 you can clearly see why.

The longer you are in this business the easier it is to find high paying people for your products.
There are many factors involved in how fast you start to make lots of money, but in the end the goal is to outsource the work and get everything on autopilot.

Let's say you find buyers who only want to pay you $100 for a per piece, don't get discouraged, with a little more research you can suddenly find high paying buyers in the thousands for your work.

And this in one product! Add that times 10 products at $1000 and you can really start to see the money pour in. Yes, some products may pay better than others, but they all add up fairly quickly in profits. You can do it all with little time and effort on your part.

Okay, you don't want $100,000 per month or year; you only want some side money, sure just work less then, research less niches, either way you are still making passive income while you sleep, its fantastic! Compare this to your standard 9 to 5 job and you start to get the idea of how profitable this business really is.
$100-$500 a day in sales is not bad if you ask me, beat that with a minimum wage standard federal level job and you get the idea.

**What the Future Holds**

The longer you stay in this business, the more success you have, you can even start a seconds business should you choose. You can even get to the point where I and many others are at the top, outsourcing your work, where everything is on autopilot.

Don't believe me, then do a simple Google search for a fellow who I am close friends with, Kindle Success Luca De Stefani, look him up on You Tube as well and type Self Publishing Revolution, he is making well over six figures a year, he coaches sure, but I am giving you the information right here free.

Once you got the hang of everything and can navigate the system like a pro, you can scale up and pass all the wannabes in this business. You can target profitable niches, create headlines that sell to your potential buyers that clients love, and keep them coming back for more, and best of all, make a killing in profits from it, not bad if you ask me. Try that with Facebook ads, or creating a You Tube channel.

You must understand what clients and buyers want, and what they are buying, these clients' wants and needs are most important for your sales pitch, sure you can sell a said product that much easier or you could try to sell a book on barn owls and how to domesticate them, but if no one wants to read this you are wasting your time and money.

Later on I will show you how to build good client relationships, how to get rid of the "middle man" for more profits and much much more. . .

This isn't something that you want to jump right into from the beginning, but we will cover these key areas to get you up to speed.
This business will start to be fun as you soon shall see, you won't feel rushed and confused, and everything will feel super easy.

2.  **Most people don't know about how profitable Making Money with Amazon Really is, So there's Less Competition**

15

The really fantastic thing about Making Money with Amazon is that many have never heard of this method of making money, and lots of it. Sure, you mention Bitcoin, Facebook ads, Drop shipping and everyone will sell you a ticket or technique.

Right now there is a need for selling on Amazon and it is growing everyday, some will say "oh Make Money on Amazon is for the birds" but little do they know, this is not your usual selling on Amazon this is Amazon selling on steroids! So what this means is LESS COMPETITION, and that is all we care about.

Every business does have some healthy competition, and that is okay, but who is your competition? Well, the ones who are at my level now and where you are going to be in the next few days. I am giving you all the tools you will need to compete with me and others at the top, there's money to go around for everyone at the top.

And if you've been around this business for some time, you will always you'll know that clients hate bad products and wont buy from them again, meaning many don't know what they are doing.

However, you and I are one and the same, different but better than the rest, because you have all the insider secrets right here in your hand.

You will succeed and make a lot of money because in this book everything is here; all the how-to information, no rock was left unturned in the making of this book, and you become one of the few, making a ton of money.
You may not know much about Search Engine Optimization yet, or perhaps you know a lot, it doesn't matter because this book is going to cover everything you need to know and more.

3. **Amazon Profits and Selling has grown into a huge Market, it's Sales on Steroids!**

16

According to many reputable online U.S. Government websites dealing with labor and law, the need for selling on Amazon has been booming over the last 3 years and its growing everyday.

When I say Amazon and selling on steroids, it truly is, you literally will never be out of work, and you can't be fired either. Try to find this freedom at most 9 to 5 jobs and you'll be hard pressed to have this kind of security. And with my system, you keep making money time and time again.

I have been making steady income in this market for the last 3 years, and make no mistake it has not dropped since. I am constantly updating this manual, so you could say it is a work in progress, as a matter of fact as of this writing I just landed 8 buyers over a 24 hour period, and they all pay very well, no more writing for free or taking stupid surveys with this business.

Now you may be thinking "hey do you sell under your own name?"

I don't, in fact I use a Business name for my Amazon sales page, and it has nothing to do with my success as a best-selling seller.

When I do sales on Amazon, I use a business name, not Tim Steinberg.

I am not using my best-selling author name to get clients, however, if you are famous yourself, or you just like people to know your name on everything that is okay, either way you will find a style that suits you best. To my clients, my work is good, and who I am is irrelevant, and you should do the same.

4. **You are in charge of your own time, work wherever you want, no one on your back!**

Think of how great it would be to have so much freedom that you could literally be working next to the beach, sipping a Pina colada, getting sun in Bali and working! Amazing, isn't. I do this now, many times when I give talks on Money Machine Master Methods;

I am in a luxurious high rise suite in Dubai, or sipping wonderful coffee in Ho Chi Minh City, Vietnam. It's Spectacular! to say the least; I just open my laptop, check some emails, get new buyers, and hire my assistant through Upwork.com and BOOM! Instant cash!
Search Engine Optimization (SEO) gives you this freedom, and best of all no one is on your back, you have no one to answer to. When people ask what you do, you can simply say I am a business person, or I run my own business online. My clients are from all over the world now, at first they were sourced from the USA only, but I expanded because many countries are starting to use English now in business, they love products from the USA.

All you need is a good internet signal, a desktop or laptop computer, or if you totally outsource now and don't do your own sales anymore, a tablet and smart phone.

You make your own hours, you can be an early bird who catches the worm, or work late night with no distractions, stay at home mom? No problem, work a job already, sure knock yourself out on your own time, do you! The sky's the limit, the only thing that holds us back is the MIND. Always maintain a positive attitude.

### 5. SEO is Super Easy

This business is so easy to do, its ridiculous. Remember, don't worry I got you covered, everything in this book is all you have to know and then some.
Never typed before? don't know what Excel means, Word, SEO, Royalty payments, Direct Deposit? No problem. Everything is here.

### 6. Not Computer Savvy? No Worries

Seriously, everything is simple, and best of all once you know how to do everything you won't forget it, so sit back, relax, and take it step by step, that is what this book is all about, easy and flowing. There is no guesswork, its not stocks.

Basically, what you need to be up and running is a basic email account, this can be who you like, Google, Yahoo, MSN, doesn't matter; next you'll need a computer, whether it be a laptop, or desktop is not important, and yes internet access.

Later on, when you get to my level, you should think about outsourcing task, such as researching your own products, finding buyers, answering emails, and so on, you can even open your own website if you want to get even more clients, opening your own website is not necessary, I don't do this, but I know some other SEO Amazon sellers who do, it doesn't matter.

Don't be put off by thinking this is all going to be a lot of work, its not, trust me. You don't need experience in this business at all. Later on should you choose to want to open a website I will show you the best and cheapest way to do this in the coming chapters.

**Action Plan**

Don't worry if you can't type, I won't ask you to take classes or anything.

Just get familiar with Microsoft Word, email, surf the net, get comfortable at first with going online, then everything will feel like a breeze.

**Summary**

There is major potential in this business for making a ton of money, in the hundreds of thousands of dollars, and best of all there is low competition, as many are not familiar with SEO Amazon sales for money. The freedom to work when and how you like is totally up to you, never again will anyone be on your back, no boss to answer to, and this is in short making money with Amazon on steroids.

Now if you are as excited as I am about how much money you are going to make, we will get started in the next chapter, by now you got familiar with some insider knowledge of how this business runs and a lot of the language we use, coming up in the next chapter we will go over this in more detail.

# HOW TO SELL ON AMAZON IN FIVE EASY STEPS

To get started with selling on Amazon you only need five things to get started:

- A highly searched product to sell
- Amazon seller account
- Hot product listings
- Inventory Management
- Ship Order Processing

### 1. Search Products to Sell on Amazon

Sourcing profitable products to sell on Amazon has many different techniques. Some sales people on Amazon will show you the traditional business model, such as selling products that they made themselves at home, or from another country, or resales of whole goods. However, there are many sellers that reach above and beyond these traditional means and come up with very creative ways to source products.

Here are my top five easy ways to make money with Amazon.

**Arbitrage Retail**

This sounds like a real hard sounding way of speaking, "arbitrage retail?" sounds like something out of the movie Tron, it is actually a simple process. You buy products in retail stores and reduced prices and then simply resell and mark them up at higher value. Sellers (such as yourself) usually will keep an eye out for any items that they are interested in reselling that are up for clearance, either from online or from you going into the retail store. When you find a great deal you just buy it.

A lot of successful sellers on Amazon got there start this way and are making a ton of money selling and reselling clearance items as their full time job. This sounds easy, and it is, but you need to learn how to know what people want, what they are willing to fork over their money for. So a big part of being successful at selling on Amazon is research, not just any research but product research, if you are trying to sell an item that no one wants you will be wasting your time and money. With a little time you will know all the ins and outs of this business and you don't have to use your own money with arbitrage retail.

**Manufactured and Wholesale Goods and How to Resell Them**

This method is where you buy products in large quantities from a wholesale store or from the manufacture, then you simply mark the item up and sell it (side tip, be willing to come down in price if the offer is good). The cool thing about this is that you can get some pretty sweet deals on wholesale prices and that increases profits. The only bad part is that you have to buy a lot of stuff, and if you hope to sell it all or most of it, you better have your research down pat.

Sellers often have large stock that is not moving, and one of the reasons is that perhaps your price is not competitive enough. What I mean by this is that usually sellers will have a good price when listing the item on Amazon, but they fail to check what other sellers are offering, is it high or low priced, on sale? For how long? All these things are important when making profits and sales.

One software I recommend and use now (no, I am not affiliated with them) is BQOOL, this software will reprice an item automatically and check to see what other sellers are doing, and if they change their price listing Bqool will detect this and change yours to out rank them. BQool also will look at profit margins and other helpful listing data.

Try them for 14 days and see if you like it, but be sure to take not of when you joined and cancel at least 3 business days before the trial is over to get a refund. The 3 days is not necessary, but I always do this to ensure full refund from businesses.

Type this link in your browser to get it now!

bit.ly/BQool14dayTrial

**Private Labeled Products**

This technique is very profitable with Amazon sellers. You purchase products from sellers as a Private Label Seller, then you add your own brand to the product(s). This works because you actually are building your brand, and like Burger King "Have it Your Way." The private label method works; you can add your own brand and label to any product, from toys, makeup, home goods and more.

Again when reselling items, you do have to purchase items in bulk, which will cost you a little, but if you did your research well on the items, then you shouldn't take that much of a loss and gain much more.

**Having Your Own Product Made**

If you already have an idea of what is selling well on Amazon or if you are already making a product yourself, then what you need to understand is Amazon's fees as a seller, and make sure you can sell it.
Amazon Seller Ranges

bit.ly/Amazonsellerfees

**Handmade Amazon Seller Fees**

sellercentral.amazon.com

**Drop Shipping**

Drop shipping has been getting a lot of attention lately, everyone thinks they know what it means, but many are sadly mistaken and often lose money in the process. Drop shipping products with Amazon is an easy and great way to make money, but if you know how to do it right.

Drop shipping is where you list an item on Amazon and put it up for sale, then the customer orders it and you 'Dropship' the product or item to a dropship vendor who ships it out for you, then you may be charged a small fee. There are some drawbacks to this method though.

Drop shipping stuff to sell has a low profit ability when you factor in Amazon's fees for the seller (you). Another potential drawback is that customers can complain, you could run out of the product, shipment was late, these are things that you really can't control that much. Not to make you think that you can't make money with Drop shipping, you can, in fact if you can find a good drop shipper that meets Amazon requirements the this method is for you.

**Take Note of Your Product Profits**

It doesn't matter where you buy and source the products you sell online at Amazon; I know that doesn't sound that great, as some countries do sell questionable items at a bargain price. You are just going to have to use your best discretion when purchasing these products. Another thing to keep in mind is that products that sell well on your site or anywhere else may take a dive when trying to sell it on Amazon. You always have to just have a quick look at Amazon seller fees just to have an idea of what profits will be coming your way.

To help you get started you can use Amazon's profit calculator, the really neat thing about this is that it will estimate your profits, and if you are into selling or have a store up already you can use this tool to look up products and see what the competition is like, this will help you save money, combine this with a profit app like BQool and you're good to go.

bit.ly/proftcalculator

When you get to the point where you know what is profitable and what type of products really sell, and you have a source that you can buy for cheap, then it is time to decide which Amazon seller account is right for you.

## 2. Set up Your Amazon Seller Account in a Flash

There are two types of Amazon Seller accounts that you can choose from. One is an Individual Seller account and the other is a Pro Seller account.

The Individual Seller Account has no monthly fees, but has 99 cents per items fee. The Pro Account is $39.99 a month, but has more perks and features over the Individual account. Both will pay for product fees on sales of items.

**bit.ly/accountstartup**

A lot of sellers go for the Pro Seller account, because of it's extra perks, it also boasts drive sales functions. To start out I would go with the Individual Seller account as you can always upgrade later once you know the system a little better.

However, if you have a lot of money to invest, and are thinking wholesale or products with private label then I would go with the Pro Seller account.

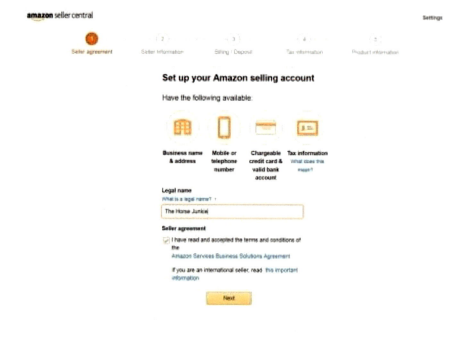

To setup your Amazon Seller Account simply go to the setup page and follow the instructions. Amazon makes it super easy.

Amazon Seller Pro and Individual Setup Page
After you setup your seller account, you will have a "dashboard" which will allow you to list your products for sale on Amazon. Next we will go into just how to do that.

### 3. How to List Products on Amazon

Once you have setup your Amazon Seller account the next step is to list your products, you can do this in many ways, but I found the most efficient and fast way is done in two steps. You simply add your items to your already existing products lists or you can create a new product list for that particular item. If you choose to add items for sale to an existing list that is the easiest way to get up and running.

**Let's start with the adding items to an existing list method first:**

Start by doing a search in Amazon to see if other sellers are already selling the product you have for sale. For example say you want to sell a bracelet and another seller already has it listed, let's take a look

When you first take a look at what you want to sell and see that another seller has it up already can make you feel like you won't make any money if you try to sell the same item, one thing to keep in mind is that although they are selling it as well, they may have low stock, or they may

stop selling it within 48 hours, this happens all the time, and guess what? They will buy from you and Amazon as soon as a seller stops selling an item, they will automatically list your item at the top for buyers to see as the next available purchase.

There are other neat things you can do as well to boost sales, you can list the price much lower than your competitor, offer free shipping to the buyer.

When you want to manually add your product to one of your seller lists it is easy in your Amazon Seller Dashboard. You start by searching the item by name under "List New Product" then type the name of the product and/or product name, product ID or SKU.

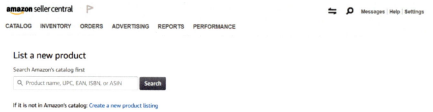

If what you want to sell is already on Amazon, you will see the product show up in the existing listings when you go to the next screen.

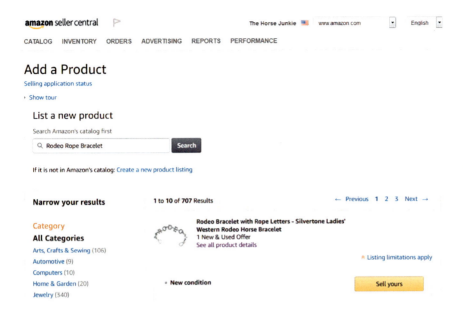

Click the orange box that says **"sell yours"** and then add your product information, the price, quantity, and fill out the rest when asked, some boxes are optional.

**Rodeo Bracelet with Rope Letters - Silvertone Ladies' Western Rodeo Horse Bracelet** (View amazon detail page)

**ASIN:** B075SPF8VD
**Product Name:** Rodeo Bracelet with Rope Letters - Silvertone Ladies' Western Rodeo Horse Bracelet
**Manufacturer:** CJW Designs
**Category (Item-type):** bracelets
**Brand Name:** The Horse Junkie
**Material Type:** NA
**Metal Type:** alloy
**Gem Type:** NA

**Marketplace:** US

**List Price:** $32.50

**Competing Marketplace Offers**
**1 New** from $22.95 + $4.99 shipping

⚠ **Offer**                                                            Advanced View ☐

| * Your price ⓘ | Lowest price for **New** |
|---|---|
| | $22.95 + $4.99 shipping   Match Low Price |
| | $ [ Ex. 58.00 ] |
| | + $4.99 shipping |

| Seller SKU ⓘ | [ Ex. 101MyCollectible1 ] |
|---|---|
| Sale Price ⓘ | $ [ Ex. 214.99 ] |
| Sale Start Date ⓘ | 📅 |
| Sale End Date ⓘ | 📅 |
| * Quantity | [                    ] |
| Condition | New ⇕ |
| Condition Note ⓘ | Condition Notes are not accepted for products with a condition type of new. |

| Manufacturer's Suggested Retail Price ⓘ | $ [ Ex. 219.99 ] |
|---|---|
| Handling Time ⓘ | [ ] |
| Restock Date | 📅 |
| Offering Can Be Gift Messaged ⓘ | ☐ |
| Is Gift Wrap Available ⓘ | ☐ |
| Max Order Quantity ⓘ | [ ] |
| Start selling date | 📅 |
| Fulfillment Channel | ⦿ I want to ship this item myself to the customer if it sells. |
| | ○ I want Amazon to ship and provide customer service for my items if they sell. Learn more |

**SHIPPING OPTIONS**

| | Transit Time | Shipping credit * | Amazon fees (if sold)* | Total you will receive* |
|---|---|---|---|---|
| Std US Dom | ☑ 4 - 14 business days | $4.99 | | |
| Std US Dom Plus | ☐ 3 - 5 business days  Example: Qualified sellers have the option to offer reduced shipping times. Learn more | | | |
| Exp US Dom | ☐ 2 - 6 business days | | | |
| Exp US Dom Plus | ☐ 1 - 3 business days  Example: Qualified sellers have the option to offer reduced shipping times. Learn more | | | |

*If Sold
All sellers are required to offer at least standard shipping. When your product sells, you will receive a shipping credit as shown. The shipping rates set by Amazon vary by product type.

[ Cancel ]   [ Save and finish ]                          Advanced View ☐

After you fill out everything and it looks good, then click on **save and finish**. Your product will be up and ready for sale, and you're good to go. Next up we will go over some things you should know when adding product listings to already existing listings in Amazon.

**Try to look for the best listing**

When you search you might find multiple lists for the exact same product you want to sell. Just look for the top ranked list and the one that has the really nice catchy images. If you add to a lot of listings this can create some friction so you need to keep an eye out on your numbers.

**Keeping an Eye on Price Matching and Profits**

Once you add your item for sale to a existing list on Amazon, then you will have a lot of competition with sales. I like to use BQool as this is what a lot of the high earner Amazon Sellers do, you can reprice and monitor what your competition is doing. BQool has a automatic repricer and when a competitor changes their prices, then yours will be reset as well, you just set it and forget it, and you are now the big competitor.

**Use Prime to Sell More**

When you want to sell on Amazon as a seller then a really neat trick is to use Prime-eligible, you will notice on sales pages in Amazon that sellers will use Prime, these sellers will also use Fulfillment by Amazon or FBA for short to ship their products.

**Pro Amazon Seller Tips to Get Started**

Now if you are a Pro Seller and have that account, then you can also add your new products to lists on Amazon manually or through what is know as the method in bulk.

**How to Create Products Listing Manually**

With Amazon Pro Seller accounts you can create a new product listing, if the item is not already sold on Amazon however don't let this deter you from the next step. It will take a little more time to add to existing lists, but you can create highly great quality lists that sell by using the power of your keyword research, niche research, product for sale competitor pictures they use, and item description, is it catchy? Is it too long? Straight to the point? You have to see why this product list is a best seller.

**Using the Method in Bulk to Manage and Add Listings**

With your Pro Seller account, you can also add your products to listings all at once by linking your items from your own website if you have one, or method in bulk using a Microsoft Excel spreadsheets and CSV files.

**Method in Bulk using Microsoft Excel Spreadsheet**

To add products to existing lists in your account, use the method in bulk. To get started you need to create a data file using Microsoft Excel,

You will upload the CSV file at this link below

bit.ly/filetemplates

Create the spreadsheet with Excel then save the CSV file, and go to the link above and upload it in your Amazon Central Dashboard.
Amazon will allow you numerous category template upload choices to choose from. Take your time, this can get a little frustrating when first trying to get everything down and can seem confusing, don't worry about it, if you are having serious trouble, and you just don't get it, then you can head on over to Upwork.com, they have virtual assistants that can help you with anything you need to do, Excel, Amazon Seller help, you name it, they can do it, and it's real cheap, say $5.00 total for the job.

bit.ly/2DBgtn0

**Product Feed Listing Method**

If you already have an Amazon Seller account, or you run your own website or both, then you can use what is known as ecommerce stores to make adding and product maintenance a breeze.

Below are some of the best Ecommerce Programs to get you Up and Running

| Site | Helps With | Cost |
|------|-----------|------|
| **Shopify**<br>**bit.ly/shopifyaccount** | Works with your own website and Amazon Seller accounts | From $29/mo. |
| **Big Commerce**<br>**bit.ly/bigacct** | Sellers that have their own site or use Amazon, Ebay | From $29.95/mo. |
| **ecomdash.com**<br>**bit.ly/ecomacct** | streamline and list products on Amazon | From $50/mo. |
| **sellbrite.com**<br>**bit.ly/sellbriteacct** | Amazon Seller Account holders, ecommerce sellers | From $230/mo. |

This is nice if you plan to make product listings in Amazon, but after you do this you will need to manage the inventory, so let's get started. . .

### 4. How to Do Inventory Management in Your Amazon Account

Doing inventory management of your account is crucial to the profitability of your sales. Amazon can and will lower your seller rating for not shipping an order in a timely fashion. Whatever you can do always be on the look out to make your inventory up to date so your Amazon seller ratings can be high.

**How to Adjust Your Inventory Yourself the Easy Way**

Log into your account and pull up your Amazon Account dashboard inventory screen, from here you can adjust the units for sale, (refer to photo), if you only have less that ten items for sale this step shouldn't take long at all.

Once you have all your Amazon listings up and running, and the inventory is good to go, then its show time as the money starts to come in from sales. The next step is to get those hot products of yours out to buyers fast, let's see just how to do this.

## 5. Amazon Orders

The final step in becoming a best seller on Amazon is shipping orders. In business one thing to keep in mind always is that everything is about the customer. There is a saying that the customer comes first and this is true in every aspect if you ever hope to be a great seller on Amazon.

Amazon expects you as the seller to fill your orders and do it with urgency, if you fail this task Amazon your Seller Rating will go down. To be successful at this you need to ship orders fast, or if it gets to be too much hire an assistant to get the job done. Remember, you can't do everything yourself once you get to the top, all businesses run this way.

**How to Ship Orders by Yourself with FBM (Fulfillment by Merchant).**

When I first started out selling on Amazon, I shipped all my orders myself, there is no shame in that, it doesn't mean you are not in the big leagues of selling on Amazon. In fact, many big name companies do this all the time, they have a warehouse where they can ship their items from and they are very successful. A lot of ecommerce do this as well by shipping all their Amazon orders directly. This is Fulfillment by Merchant (FBM).

So, you are ready to take the plunge and do it yourself, okay if you never shipped before, no problem, Amazon likes to help every step of the way. You really have two options to offer the buyer, free shipping and charging for shipping, it's up to you, but keep in mind that free shipping will get you more buys, but it's your call. Also you can get orders printed up with the United States Postal Service or UPS. In your Amazon Seller account you can print labels in your dashboard.

Plus, you can print orders and print both US Postal and UPS shipping labels right from your Amazon Seller Central dashboard.

Here is a checklist of things you are going to need to get you up and running:

- Boxes for Shipping
- Sturdy Box Shipping Tape
- Filler for the Boxes, paper, bubble wrap
- A good digital shipping scale (don't try your bathroom scale, invest in a good one)
- Make it easy for your shippers to get your packages, such as ease of delivery drop off and a secure place for picking up the items.

Don't worry if everything seems overwhelming, just start small and take it step by step. Try to be fast, as Amazon likes this.

**Use Amazon to Ship and Fill Orders for You, this is called FBA (Fulfillment by Amazon)**

Here is how Fulfillment by Amazon works, you simply ship your products to Amazon, then they will pack, and you're your items for you.

There will be some small fess, but with less hassle of shipping, pick up and drop off points, etc. You have to decide if you want to take your business to the next level and free up more of your time for doing Keyword research, niche, product searching, and who your competitors are. With Amazon taking control, their services do come with some great benefits to you in making your sales go up:

- **Listing Products as Prime Eligible:** Fulfillment by Amazon items get listed as Prime Amazon Products.
- **Prime Will Drive Up Sales and More Buyers Looking at Your Products:** The latest research with Amazon buyers is that 70% of USA shoppers on Amazon are in fact Prime Members. And this totals to $90 million buyers in 2017 alone, which means they are looking for Prime Products to buy.

- **Prime Buyers get Free Shipping:** With Fulfillment by Amazon you make your products eligible for 2-day free shipping.
- **Your Product Listings Rank Higher:** When you use Amazon's FBA option they give you higher ranking automatically because it sets off their algorithm which is unique to Amazon much like Google's algorithm.
- **You Get More Box Buy Listings:** If prices are the same, Fulfillment by Amazon has the Buy Box option.
- **Buyers Trust FBA:** Buyers know when they see FBA on a product they are in good hands, and they trust that all will go well with shipping and timeliness. This means more sales for you.
- **Your Sales Will Go Up with FBA:** With all these perks it is no wonder a lot of the top sellers including myself go with Fulfillment by Amazon for their business needs.

If you choose to use FBA, what is good to know is that you can rise above the competition fast! Because many don't want to take the plunge with letting Amazon do the work.

When you use FBA you need to know a few more things. When you send your goods to Amazon they go to their warehouse and you need not worry what happens there, you're in good hands. Here is a quick checklist for using this service to make things easier:

- Print a barcode for labels
- Packaging items, bags

How often you will have to do this depends on how big your operation is, if you are starting small as a seller, say shipping twice a month, or only one time, then filling orders everyday, can't get hard as you scale up in your business and start making a lot of money. Amazon shipping costs are cheap so your cost will be low.

**How About if I use a Third Party Partner To Do What FBA does?**

Sounds nice, I don't recommend this, as Amazon makes it super easy anyway and cheaper in costs to you, and you get the rankings and sales drive as well, but if you have a source that is cheaper than Amazon and can do what they do or better, then go for it.

In the end, if you are starting our small, don't worry about it, just get your feet wet, learn the ropes, and take it step by step. In other words, don't try to reinvent the wheel.

Type this link in your browser to get started:

**bit.ly/FBAamazonacct**

## How to Make Money with Amazon

Amazon is the future and is here to stay; the potential to make money is high. Many will say the market is saturated and the competition is too stiff. I don't listen to naysayers, there is room for everybody. One thing for sure Amazon Sellers is in high demand, and it isn't going to stop any time soon.

# HOME IMPROVEMENT

The first area that we will focus on is home improvement, but why, what is it about this niche that attracts so many buyers. You have to think like a buyer, people are always buying items to build and improve their home. Start by searching the items listed in Amazon and you will see customer reviews and if it is a best seller or not. This niche is here to stay, and there is a ton of money in it, trust me.

**Power Tools and Various Items for Home Improvement:**

**Ingersoll Rand Drill**

**Ingersoll Rand 2235TiMAX Drive Air Impact Wrench, 1/2 Inch**

Product Specs:

- 1/2-inch air impact wrench delivers up to 1,350 foot-pounds of nut-busting torque
- Compact, lightweight design weighs only 4.6 pounds and keeps fatigue to a minimum
- 4-position power regulator lets you easily adjust torque output on the fly
- Twin-hammer mechanism for maximum power and longevity
- Rugged housing, titanium hammer case, and steel wear plate for exceptional durability

This item can easily be found on Amazon.

**PORTER-CABLE C2002-WK Oil-Free UMC Pancake Compressor with 13-Piece Accessory Kit**
Product Specs:

- Constructed with a pancake style tank for optimal stability
- Provides longer air tool performance
- Contains a 6 gallon capacity
- Includes 13 piece accessory kit
- 150 psi max tank pressure stores more air in the tank for longer tool run times
- 2.6 SCFM at 90 psi allows for quick compressor recovery time, per ISO1217
- Air coupler and plug are factory installed on the air hose to save user labor and to prevent leaks

## Ingersoll-Rand 232TGSL 1/2-Inch Super-Duty Air Impact Wrench Thunder Gun

Product Specs:
- Plastic / Metal
- Imported
- Distinctive appearance, similar to IR Thunder Gun racing tool
- Adjustable power regulator
- The Ingersoll-Rand fastest 1/2-inch impact wrench available
- 625-feet-per-pound of maximum reverse torque; 550-feet-per-pound of forward torque
- Weighs 6-pounds

## Senco PC1010 1-Horsepower Peak, 1/2 hp running 1-Gallon Compressor

Product Specs:

- Lightweight and portable--easy to carry from site to site as you work
- One horsepower peak ,1/2 horsepower running and one-gallon capacity
- Ideal for a range of renovation and home improvement jobs, as well as for hobbies and crafts
- Delivers 20 to 44 drives per minute

- Backed by a one-year warranty

**Ingersoll-Rand 2135TiMAX 1/2-Inch Air Impact Wrench**

Product Specs:
- 780-foot-pounds max power
- New professional touch trigger with a wider range of power regulator settings in forward
- Patented push button forward/reverse provides maximum control
- Weighs just 3.95-pounds
- Designed to last and backed by the MAX Protection Program that offers a free 2 year limited warranty with tool registration
-

**Ingersoll Rand 231C Super-Duty Air Impact Wrench, 1/2 Inch**

Product Specs:
- Metal / Plastic
- Imported
- Classic, reliable design offers proven power, performance, and durability
- Twin-hammer mechanism delivers a maximum torque of 600 foot-pounds
- Adjustable power regulator provides easy control of torque output
- Ergonomic 2-piece design is easy to operate and maintain
- Arrives fully lubricated and ready for use out of the box

This niche is great because there are endless customers for home improvement tools.

Customers in this niche are mostly people with disposable income, and as I stated before people will always need to do home improvement and these and more items will be in demand.

These customers will always repeat purchase, which is good for you.

# HOME APPLIANCES, ARTS AND CRAFTS AND HOW TO GET INVOLVED AND MAKE MONEY

Home appliances is a great niche because the sales are tremendous when it comes to holiday, gifts, weddings, you name it, no matter what occasion this niche delivers.

**Danby 120 Can Beverage Center, Stainless Steel DBC120BLS**

Product Specs:

- 3.3 cu. ft. capacity beverage center (up to 120 cans)
- Mechanical thermostat with temperature range of 43F - 57F
- 3 black wire shelves and interior light illuminates compartment when door is opened
- Recessed side mount door handle and integrated lock with key. Tempered glass door with stainless steel trim and black body
- Please refer Pages 5-7 in user manual under technical specification for the installation and troubleshooting guide.

**SPT Countertop Dishwasher, White**

Product Specs:
- Durable stainless steel interior and spray arm
- Dish rack and silverware basket; up to 6 standard place settings capacity
- User friendly controls; automatic detergent and rinse agent dispenser
- Faucet adapter included for quick and simple connection
- 6 wash cycles (heavy, normal, light, glass, speed, soak); Unit dimension (W x D x H) : 21.65 x 19.69 x 17.24 in

**Panda Small Compact Portable Washing Machine 7.9lbs Capacity with Spin Dryer**

Product Specs:

- Small Portable washing machine goes anywhere with only 28lbs weight
- Easy to operate, and powerful Just fill with water and set timer
- Perfect for Apartments, Dorms, RV, Travel, your second washer at home
- One side of washing, one side of spinning

**SPT 2.5 cu.ft Compact Refrigerator Stainless Door with Black Sides**
Product Specs:

- 2.5 cu.ft. net capacity with adjustable thermostat and HCFC free
- Reversible door with slide out wire shelf for storage versatility
- Estimated yearly operating cost: $28 based on 10.65 cent per kwh 2007
- Transparent vegetable storage drawer with glass shelf

**Midea WHS-185C1 Single Door Chest Freezer, 5.0 Cubic Feet, White**

Product Specs:

- Small Portable washing machine goes anywhere with only 28lbs weight
- Easy to operate, and powerful Just fill with water and set timer
- Perfect for Apartments, Dorms, RV, Travel, your second washer at home
- One side of washing, one side of spinning

This niche is great because there are endless customers for home appliances.

Many buyers want appliances and need them

Home appliances are fabricated quite quickly, making this niche very lucrative.

Buyers in this niche will be very affluent when it comes to buying appliances.

# THE BIG MONEY MAKER WITH ARTS AND CRAFTS

This niche is great because there are endless customers for Arts and Crafts.

Buyers love to keep busy and make stuff, so you can bet you're making endless cash on this niche.

All kinds of machines and gadgets are always being updated and someone makes a new type of this or that one, no matter to us we just want to make that money, and make a customer happy.
Arts and Crafts niches always will have repeat customers and are always needed.

**Brother cs6000i 60-Stitch Computerized Sewing Machine with Wide Table**

Product Specs:

- Versatile, value-packed, perfect for a wide range of sewing and quilting projects, accessories are stored inside a compartment on the arm of the sewing machine
- Select stitches and adjust stitch length and stitch width via settings seen on the LCD display
- Stop/start button allows use without included foot control. Variable speed control for easily adjusting your sewing speed
- Jam-resistant Quick-set top drop-in bobbin makes setting and accessing your bobbin thread a breeze. No more fishing for your bobbin thread. Accessories are stored in a compartment on the arm of the machine.

- Bilingual user manual, 25-year limited warranty, and free phone support for the life of the product. We do not recommend using this machine in countries that do not support 120V AC even if a voltage adapter is in use
- Included Accessory Feet: Buttonhole foot, Overcasting foot, Monogramming foot, Zipper foot, Zigzag foot, Blind stitch foot, Button fitting foot, Walking foot, Spring action quilting foot Other, Included Accessories : Accessory pouch with needle set, twin needle, spool pin, bobbins (3), cleaning brush, seam ripper, screwdriver, eyelet punch, power cord, Operation Manual, hard protective case, oversized table

## Silhouette Cameo Starter Bundle (Old Model)

Product Specs:

- The silhouette cameo starter bundle includes an extra mat
- (2 total), cutting blade (2 total), metallic pen set and pick-me-up-tool
- 50 exclusive cuttable designs.
- Includes access to thousands of downloadable designs; Includes PC and Mac compatible software, One month free subscription ($10 value, gray card located in accessory tray) is included for use at the Silhouette Online Store.
- Cuts up to 12-inch wide and 10-feet long; cuts a variety of materials from vinyl to fabric . Does not Include Starter Kit vinyl
- Great for Scrapbook layouts, cards, custom apparel, vinyl decor, etched glass, sketch designs, and paper crafts

## SINGER 4423 Heavy Duty Model Sewing Machine

Product Specs:

- 23 built-in stitches: 6 basic stitches, 4 stretch stitches, 12 decorative stitches, 1 Buttonhole

- Automatic needle threader; top drop-in bobbin
- 1,100 stitches per minute; 60Percent stronger motor
- Stainless steel bed plate; heavy duty metal Frame; Snap-On Presser feet
- Fully automatic 1-step Buttonhole: make beautiful buttonholes automatically in 1 easy step
- Extra-High Sewing Speed of 1,100 stitches per minute gives you professional speed for faster results
- Heavy Duty Interior Metal Frame ensures that the machine remains still for skip-free sewing.

**Sizzix 655268 Big Shot Cutting-and-Embossing Roller-Style Machine with Standard Multipurpose Platform, Black & Pink**

Product Specs:

- Older version Pink & Black Big Shot with Standard Platform; replaced by New Powder Blue & Teal Big Shot with Extended Multipurpose Platform
- Portable shape-cutting and embossing roller-style machine accommodates a wide range of crafting materials from paper to fabric
- Works with almost the entire Sizzix product library, as well as other die-cutting and embossing tools
- Includes multipurpose platform and a pair of standard cutting pads
- Measures approximately 14-1/4 by 12-3/8 by 6-5/8 inches

Amazon Page for Ideas on Products and Niches to jump into

# The Women's Jewelry Niche

I had to devote a whole chapter, to Women's Jewelry, don't worry it will be short. Reason being is because this is a great way to make money; it's a beautiful niche that attracts millions. You ever watch the late night infomercials, or the shopping channel where there selling fine jewelry and other dazzling items, you must have thought "hey I could make money doing that, but how? Ah forget it" well I'm here to tell you this niche is exploding, below are some of the hottest items selling on Amazon now, so let's get started.

**Bella beat Leaf Nature Health Tracker/Smart Jewelry, Silver Edition**

Product Specs:

- American White Ash wood
- Imported
- *NOTE: All users, In order to sync the Leaf with phone, make sure to turn on your Bluetooth and to press the SYNC icon in the app and then keenly follow the user guide and troubleshooting guide
- Tracks your steps, distance moved and calories burned
- Tracks your sleep patterns, revealing the quantity and quality of your sleep. Tracks your reproductive health, providing you with an overview of your menstrual cycle
- Monitors your stress levels and helps you manage and relieve stress through goal-oriented breathing exercises
- Wakes you gently in the morning and reminds you to stay active with Inactivity Alarm

**Bella beat Leaf Nature Health Tracker/Smart Jewelry**

**Tahitian Cultured Black Pearl Pendant Necklace 9-10mm Round Sterling Silver Anniversary Gifts for Women – Viki Lynn**

Product Specs:

- VIKI LYNN: This is a stunning 9-10mm round Tahitian cultured pearl necklace that is not only high quality, but reflects a mysterious and elegant luster when worn. This pearl pendant is made of 925 sterling silver, is +18k gold plated, whose silver part is not oxidized easily, remaining radiant.
- This fabulous Tahitian Pearl Necklace is the ultimate jewelry for women, Christmas Gifts for women, Mothers day gifts for mom , Birthday gifts for women, Wedding Anniversary Gifts for her, Gifts for wife or simply, "Just Because", ensuring a smile on your loved one's face.
- Attention please: Most Tahitian pearls that are identified as "black" are actually charcoal grey, silver, or dark green. Each Tahitian Black Pearl has an official certification.
- Pendant size: 2.5 1.1cm, weight 3.5 grams, comes with a free 18 inch 925 sterling silver chain.

Pearls are a chemical and an organic gem that require specialized care. They deteriorate in contact with chemicals like household cleaners, perfumes, cosmetics, and any hair care product of all kinds. A good rule of thumb is that your pearls are "The Last Thing You Put On", when dressing, and "The First Thing You Take Off", when you get home. The surface of a pearl is soft and can be easily damaged, store it inside a well made jewelry box for safe keeping.

**14K Gold White Freshwater Cultured Pearl Necklace, 18" Princess Length**

Product Specs

- All Freshwater Pearls are directly imported from the pearl farms of China. Our pearls represent the finest in pearl selection, handpicked for its luster, quality, color, and cleanliness.
- Each Necklace is affixed with the highest quality 14K gold clasp. The option is given to select either white or yellow gold based on your preferences.
- Only the most elegant jewelry boxes are used to package and ship our necklaces, ensuring the most beautiful presentation possible. Additionally, all products are accompanied with a genuine cultured pearl guarantee, verifying the quality and source of the pearls.

To guarantee your complete and total satisfaction, we offer our customers a 60-Day return policy.

The Pearl Source has been nominated as one of the few Top Holiday sellers in the Jewelry category on Amazon, and we continue to rank among the top companies for customer satisfaction and the best shopping experience. Furthermore, The Pearl Source is one of the only leading Foundation Members of the cultured Pearl Association of America (CPAA) on Amazon.

**14k Yellow Gold Solid Polished Cross Pendant Necklace, 18"**

Product Specs

- 14k yellow gold classic solid polished cross.
- A beautiful, classic, timeless design.
- Spring ring clasp.
- Hand crafted in the USA.

**14k Diamond with Screw Back and Post Stud Earrings (J-K Color, I2-I3 Clarity)**

Product Specs

- Classic solitaire studs featuring diamonds nestled in four-prong settings and screw-on backings
- Carat weight listed is the total for both studs
- All our diamond suppliers confirm that they comply with the Kimberley Process to ensure that their diamonds are conflict free
- Made in United States

**AGS Certified 1/3 Carat Round Diamond Solitaire Pendant in 14K White Gold (K-L Color, I2-I3 Clarity)**

Product Specs

- 14k White gold
- Gem Type: White Diamond
- Setting: Solitaire
- Length 18 inches
- AGS Certified 1/3 Carat Round Diamond Solitaire Pendant in 14K White Gold

This niche is great because there are endless customers for Jewelry.

Women's jewelry is a niche that makes money fast, and its growing by the day.

Women as well as men go crazy for jewelry and they make great gifts, holidays, weddings, and so on the profits are endless.
This niche is fantastic and one of my personal favorites.

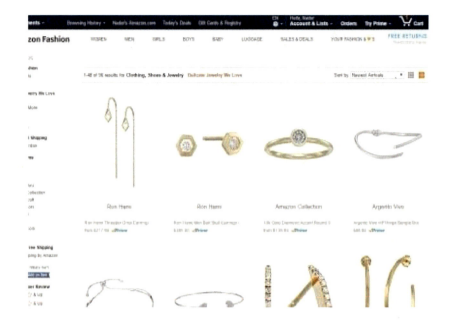

Various Jewelry that Sell Well on Amazon

# AUTOMOTIVE PARTS NICHE

This niche is awesome because auto parts and accessories are a must, all the do it yourself types are willing to spend the money on repair. You can sure bet there are endless opportunities to make money with this nice.

**Tekonsha 90195 P3 Electronic Brake Control**

Product Specs:

- A distinct, easy-to-read LCD display with multiple screen color options, displays in English, French or Spanish
- Diagnostics show output current, battery, brake, and output voltage and warning system alerts to No Trailer Brake situations
- Boost feature allows for different levels of customized braking, select Electric over Hydraulic or Electric trailer brake mode
- Integrated Plug-N-Play port for 2-plug adapters and Snap-in mounting clip allows user to remove and store the control when not in use

**Royal Purple 05130 API-Licensed SAE 10W-30 High Performance Synthetic Motor Oil - 5 gal.**
Product Specs:

- Better wear protection
- Increased fuel efficiency
- Better protection of the expensive catalytic emission system
- Improved compatibility with fuels containing ethanol
- Superior corrosion protection

**Mobil 1 98KG00 0W-40 Synthetic Motor Oil - 1 Quart**

Product Specs:

- Active cleaning agents to prevents deposits and sludge build-up to enable long and clean engine life
- Outstanding thermal and oxidation stability to reduces oil ageing allowing extended drain interval protection
- Low oil consumption and less hydrocarbon pollution
- Enhanced frictional properties for greater fuel economy
- Excellent low temperature capabilities for quick cold weather starting and ultra fast protection for extended engine and electrical system life

**Red Line 50304-12PK Manual Transmission (MT) 90W Gear Oil - 1 Quart, (Pack of 12)**
- Product Specs:
- Easier shifting.
- Extra gear protection
- Good shift ability and synchro compatibility
- Provides proper shifting over the entire temperature range
- Shear stability and oxidation stability!

**Delphi FJ10566 Fuel Injector SCPI to MFI Conversion Assembly**

Product Specs:

- Accurate, tightly controlled fuel spray pattern for more efficient fuel vaporization, reducing unburned hydrocarbon emissions
- Internal seal rings protected from fuel exposure, minimizing in-use "sticking" for longer-lasting durability
- Improved sealing materials, providing cold sealing to -40 degrees C for better cold starts
- Multi Fuel capability
- 

This niche is great because there are endless customers for automotive parts.

It is very profitable with a lot of material and products being sold and made.
Many buyers love automotive accessories and they are happy to buy again.

This niche sells at high cost which is good for you.

# POWERED GAS / ELECTRIC OPERATED BIKES

These are really cool gifts for the hubby or for anyone, Christmas and more. The profits are endless for this niche. This niche is great because there are endless customers for Gas Powered Bikes.

Buyer potential is extremely high with this niche.

Buyers need to upgrade, buy parts and are always on the lookout for a deal, which means more money for you.

These bikes always have newer models coming out, which means more buyer money for you.

**Coleman CT200U Trail200 Gas-Powered Mini Bike**

Product Specs:

- Coleman CT200U Trail200 Gas-Powered Mini Bike
- Age Range:12 to 14 Years
- Maximum Weight:200 lbs.
- Color: Red
- Gender: Boys ,Girls
- Manufacturer Part Number:CT200U
- Brand: Coleman

**Coleman Power sports CT200U Gas Powered Mini Trail Bike**

Product Specs:

- 4 stroke OHV 1 cylinder - 196cc/6.5hp engine
- Easy pull start operation; Low pressure tires for soft ride

- Sturdy metal frame and racks
- Rear Drum - handle operated braking system
- Racks not included

**Xtreme power US 40CC 4-Stroke Gas Power Mini Pocket Motorcycle Ride-on, Blue/Black, EPA Certificated**

Product Specs:

- Ideal for driveway and parking lot fun for kids 12 years and older; Minimum recommended age: 12 year-age
- Features standard with front & rear disc brakes and large 11 inch pneumatic street tires
- Max. rider weight: 165 lbs; Max Speed18 mph; Transmission: chain drive
- Motor: 40CC 4 Stroke EPA Approval; Fuel/Oil: >#90; Gas Tank: 1.2 liters; Cruising Range: 42 km per tank
- Overall Dimension: (L x W x H) 40" x 18.5" x 22.8"; Brakes: 1 disc front, 1 disc rear

# FANTASTIC ELECTRIC BIKES

**Razor MX650 Rocket Electric Motocross Bike**

Product Specs:

- Compact electric motocross bike with powerful 650-watt electric motor
- Carries riders at speeds of up to 17 mph; authentic dirt bike frame geometry
- Dual suspension and riser handlebars deliver smooth, comfortable ride

- Pneumatic knobby tires for maximum power transfer; quiet variable-speed, chain-driven motor
- Recommended for ages 16 and older (220-pound weight limit); 90-day warranty

**Ancheer Power Plus Electric Mountain Bike with Removable Lithium-Ion Battery, Battery Charger**
Product Specs:

- FREE ASSEMBLY SERVICE AVAILABLE--when purchasing this e bike, click on the "Select Assembly Preference" button above, choose "Ship to store for assembly and pickup" or "At-home assembly by mobile professional".
- PREMIUM QUALITY: The e-bike adopts 100 percent aluminum alloy frame, the front fork is made of high-strength carbon steel and packed with premium comfort shock absorption; Meter has 3-speed smart meter button and double layer aluminum alloy 26 inch wheel.
- BRAKE & GEAR SHIFT SYSTEM: With front and rear disc brakes and 21-speed transmission system, you can choose any speed to complete your journey, and perfect brakes fully protect your safety. And the bright LED headlamp and horn is equipped for night riding.
- LITHIUM BATTERY & HIGH SPEED MOTOR: The removable 36V, 8AH Ion lithium battery, equipped with smart lithium battery charger can make you ride up to 25-50 kms. 250W high speed brushless gear motors easily assists you to travel at the 15mph road speed limit.
- WORKING MODE: E-bike & Assisted bicycle, you can choose the E-bike to enjoy a long time travel, and also exercise; combining two modes would be a better choice

**Hover-1 Folding Electric Scooter and Urban E-Bike, Electric Bike with 20 MPH Speed, 22-Mile Range**

Product Specs:

- Features R/L Dual disc brakes, a spring loaded kickstand, also comes with extra wide 10-inch pneumatic tires along with a padded seat that offers a comfortable and pleasant riding experience. Strong Metal Frame. Rear located turning light and brake light.
- Beautiful LCD Display with digital speedometer/odometer/trip-meter/headlight, temperature and battery life indicatory and more! • High-performance Brushless Motor allows max speeds of up to 20mph. Max speed riding time of 1-hour and 20 minutes. Offers a "suggested use" ride time of 2.5-3 hours.
- 285lbs weight capacity. Adult-use only - with a 14+ suggested age rating. Unique Key based system offers maximum protection from unauthorized use or theft
- Some Additional Safety features: i.e. Brake-activated power cut-off when both break and throttle mistakenly applied. Completely resettable circuits and fuses have been used to protect the overall system ensuring maintenance is kept to a minimum. Plus many more! NO ASSEMBLY REQUIRED.
- Charge in any outlet, anywhere, typical charge times range between 3-5 hours. Product Size (unfolded): 42.24" H x 37.5" L x 21.2" D Product Size (Folded): 45" H x 21.3" L x 11" D

**SWAGTRON SwagCycle E-Bike – Folding Electric Bicycle with 10 Mile Range, Collapsible Frame, and Handlebar Display**

Product Specs:

- 10 MPH & 10 MILE RANGE - The motorized bicycle uses a 36v battery & a 250-watt motor that charges in 2.5 hours.
- COLLAPSES FOR EASY STORAGE - The folding bike uses an aerospace grade aluminum frame & easily fits in trunks of all sizes.

- HANDLEBAR DISPLAY – Check battery life, turn on the headlight, honk the horn, accelerate, & brake all from the handlebars.
- CHARGE YOUR DEVICES ON THE GO – A micro USB charging port enables you to charge your devices while you ride.
- ZERO EMISSIONS – The eco-friendly Swagger is 100% electric & emissions free, saving both your wallet & the environment.

**Razor RSF650 Street Bike**

Product Specs:

- Powered by a 650 watt high-torque, chain-driven motor on a steel trellis-frame Chassis design and street geometry with low profile windscreen
- Features custom 12 inch 10-spoke mag wheels and street tires, rear suspension, Variable speed twist-grip throttle, and hand-operated rear disc brakes
- 36V (three 12V) sealed lead acid Rechargeable battery with quick-change compartment and up to 50 minutes of continuous use
- Also, includes adjustable angle riser style handlebars, soft rubber grips, retractable kickstand, folding foot pegs, and Hidden storage compartment
- Recommended for ages 16 and up; supports riders up to 220 pounds

**AW 26 "x1.75" Rear Wheel 48V 1000W Electric Bicycle Motor Kit E-Bike Cycling Hub Conversion Dual Mode Controller**

Product Specs:

- The kit includes motorized wheel, motor controller, speed throttle, power break lever, wire harness

- 45 - 48 KM/H top speed, Motor specifications: 48v / 1000w / 470rpm
- Drive system has no moving chains or gears, no friction, more efficient, less chance to break!
- Dual Mode Controller: Motor works under Hall effect and non-Hall effect, extend life for electric bike
- Provides you with a whole wheel with tire, not just the tire frame Takes less than hour to install

**Onway 26" 750W 7 Speed Snow & Beach Fat Tire Electric Bike, All Terrain Using with Pedal Assist and Throttle**

Product Specs:

- Strong driving force: 48V 750W Bafang motor, 11.6AH SONY lithium battery, quality is up to 3 years guaranteed
- Fantastic driving experience: Shimano 7 speed gear, 20 mile/h top speed & 46 miles max distance. 4-6H charging time
- Warranty information: Details are added in description. Batteries and other accessories are provided from USA warehouse
- Easy to use: Adjustable seat suits for any rider. 9-level assist LCD mode display will bring you a fun riding experience
- All terrain application: 26*4.0 fat tire, apply to all terrain, can be used in sand beach and snow ground, without limitation of seasons

**ANCHEER Folding Electric Mountain Bike with 26" Super Lightweight Magnesium Alloy 6 Spokes Integrated Wheel, Large Capacity Lithium-Ion Battery (36V 250W), Premium Full Suspension and Shimano Gear**

Product Specs:

- INDUSTRY ALUMINUM ALLOY FRAME: Adopts ultra lightweight yet strong aluminum. Anti-rust and anti-exposure painting material.
- LARGE-CAPACITY LITHIUM BATTERY: 36V/8AH li battery supports 25km/15.5mile ( E-Bike Mode ) to 50km/31mile ( Assisted Mode ) ridding. Equipped with smart lithium battery charger for fast charging (4-6 hrs).
- ULTRA STRONG WHEELS: 26 inch magnesium alloy integrated wheels with anti-slip resistant thick tire-- Suit for Rainy or snowy mountain way and road way.
- BRAKE & MOTOR SYSTEM: Mechanical front and rear disc-brake design and 21-speed Shimano professional transmission system. Perfect climbing ability.
- 2 WORKING MODE: E-bike & Assisted bicycle. Meter has 3-speed smart buttons. LED front light and horn are included. Enjoy your ride with any mode! FREE ASSEMBLY SERVICE AVAILABLE--when purchasing this e bike, click on the "Select Assembly Preference" button above, choose "Ship to store for assembly and pickup" or "At-home assembly by mobile professional"

**Goplus 20" 250W Folding Electric Bike Sport Mountain Bicycle 36V Lithium Battery**
Product Specs:

- Easy Folding- Ideal for travelling holidays and those with minimal storage space
- Lithium Battery-The removable 36V, 8AH lithium battery, equipped with AMA brand motor, mobile brand battery charger can make you ride up to 25-30 kms,And it charge easily
- Charger UL approved-Charger UL approved make you safe, safeguard, feel relieved

- Adjustable Electric Bike-Allows for plenty of saddle height adjustment to suit the rider and is fitted with a quick-release clamp to assist in folding the bike quickly
- Well-made Frame-The e-bike adopts 100 percent aluminum alloy frame, the front fork is made of high-strength carbon steel and packed with premium comfort shock absorption

**Pulse Performance Products Em-1000 E-Motorcycle**

Product Specs:

- 2-wheeled electric motorcycle with 100-watt chain driven motor and speeds up to 10 mph
- Heavy-duty steel frame improves durability while puncture-proof knobby front tire and air-filled rubber rear tire absorb bumps
- Moto-inspired Instant Throttle Response (ITR) twist throttle and caliper hand brake enable superior control
- 24-volt rechargeable battery system for a continuous ride time of up to 40 minutes
- Designed for riders 8 years and older, weighing up to 120 lbs.

This niche is great because there are endless customers for Gas and Electric Powered Bikes.

Bikes are a hot gift idea and sale item for many buyers, this niche has a lot of money in it. Reason being is that these bikes take the environment into consideration and many now view going green as a way of the future.

Many buyers see these bikes as safer and saving on money for them when they need to travel, especially in affluent areas of the country, with smaller as well as bigger cities, where many don't own a car.

Gas and Electric bikes cost more than a regular bike on most cases, but these buyers are willing to pay as proven by many people's earnings in this niche.

Now I think you get the idea on how to search for items and where to post and sell, so from here on out, get used to searching through Amazon for best sellers in the niche category of your choice. I will list the items and you can save time and money of course, and dive right in.

Take your time to research each niche; don't just get into it because you think you will make fast cash. Now that may be true that you can make lots of money on many niches, I do myself, but what I mean is that we should read up on the niche of choice, check out some reviews, see what the buyers are saying, get some feedback. And I always go by gut feeling, if I like a particular niche, I go for it, regardless of what the "experts" say. Have fun!

# HOT NICHES FBA FOR MORE PROFITS

This chapter will cover many of the hot niches as of this writing, they sell well. Don't hesitate to jump right in.

**Baby Seats, Booster Seats and More**

Now remember, anyone of these I have listed can be found by going directly to Amazon.com and searching.

- Graco Nautilus Baby Seat
- Baby Booster Seat
- Pritax Pinacle Booster Seat
- Graco 4 in 1 Seating System
- Moonlight Slumber Little Dreamer
- Lotus Travel Crib

This niche is great because there are endless customers for Baby Seats and Cribs and the list goes on and on.

Babies are born every day and so the profits are endless in this niche as you can imagine.

Buyers in this niche will spend a fortune for their babies and always want the safest and most easily usable items they can think of.

The baby Niche is fantastic, doesn't matter the holiday or the season, babies products are always in high demand.

**Electronics**
- Escort Passport Radar Detector
- ASUS Wireless Router
- Pelican Protect Gun Case

This niche is great because there are endless customers for electronics.

Buyers again will be on the lookout for deals and what is cool and new. Electronics are trendy and people just want to have fun.

This niche goes off the premise of what customer's desire and what they need and want it's a really great niche.
Electronic niche is here to stay and whether is the new Apple device or the passport radar detector; you will always have a buyer.

## TVs and More

- Samsung 32-Inch TV
- Samsung Electronics 55-Inch 4K Ultra HD Smart LED TV
- 55 inch Vizomax TV Screen Protector
- Samsung Curved 55-Inch
- Samsung 55" Class
- LG Electronics 55-Inch 4K Ultra HD

This niche is great because there are endless customers for TVs and Home Systems.

Believe it or not there is a TV in almost everyone's home. More often than not, households always have some kind of a TV in it.

TV's are always in high demand, and you can always bet on a sale with a TV.

With online shopping as popular as ever, many people want the best deal they can afford, there is room for everybody.

## Speakers and Home Theatre Systems

- UE Boom Speakers
- Yamaha Front Surround System

- Orb Audio Mini 5.1 Home Theater Speaker System
- Dual LU43PB 100 Watt 3-way Indoor/Outdoor Speakers in Black (Pair)
- Edifier R1280T Powered Bookshelf Speakers - 2.0 Active Near Field Monitors - Studio Monitor

This niche is great because there are endless customers for

**Speakers and Home Theatre Systems.**

- UE Boom Speakers
- Yamaha Front Surround System
- Orb Audio Mini 5.1 Home Theater Speaker System
- Dual LU43PB 100 Watt 3-way Indoor/Outdoor Speakers in Black (Pair)
- Edifier R1280T Powered Bookshelf Speakers - 2.0 Active Near Field Monitors - Studio Monitor

Speakers are fabulous, just think of all the buyer potential, karaoke parties and more.

Good speakers come at a hefty price, but you can always bet on a sale in your favor for profits, trust me.

**Desktop and Computer Speakers**

- Klipsch ProMedia 2.1 THX Certified Computer Speaker System
- Logitech Z623 200 Watt Home Speaker System, 2.1 Speaker System
- Klipsch ProMedia 2.1 THX Certified Computer Speaker System
- Dell A525 Computer Speakers 2.1 System with Subwoofer TH760
- Creative Labs 5300 Inspire 5.1 Computer Speakers

- Arion Legacy AC Powered Studio Quality 2.0 Speakers

This niche is great because there are endless customers for

Buyers for this niche are always buying, not only do speakers enhance the user experience but they are willing to pay.

Speakers for a computer can vary from high and low end pricing so adjust accordingly when getting into this niche.

Buyers are very into this niche from my research and sales with it.

**On the go Speakers**

- ARCHEER 25W Bluetooth Speaker
- Bose Sound Link Mini Bluetooth Speaker II
- Ultimate Ears BOOM 2 Meteor Wireless Mobile Bluetooth Speaker
- FUGOO Style XL- Portable Rugged Waterproof Wireless Bluetooth Speaker
- Pyle PPHP837UB Powered Active PA System Loudspeaker Bluetooth with Microphone
- ION Audio Tailgater (iPA77) | Portable Bluetooth PA Speaker with Mic

This niche is great because there are endless customers for on the go and portable speakers.

Buyers love these because of trends and keeping up to date with being flashy and so forth, there is always potential with this nice.

Portable speakers vary in range from high quality to knockoff types, so adjust accordingly when getting into this niche, in short know what's hot and what is not.

Portable speakers are very versatile, users love these, and they can be imported or shipped to almost anywhere in the world.

**Microphones and More**

Microphones are a really cool niche, I have seen some really far out microphones when traveling in South East Asia, places like Vietnam, South Korea and others have a really cool Karaoke microphone with hundreds of songs that you can sing along too and even adjust the volume, if you see any of these jump on them fast. Below are some really cool ones I make great sales with.

- Blue Microphones Blackout Yeti USB Microphone
- Shure MV88 iOS Digital Stereo Condenser Microphone
- Audio-Technica AT2020USB
- Audio-Technica AT875R Line
- Neumann KMS 105 - Nickel
- Blue Microphones ABLMYETISGK1 Yeti USB Microphone
- Audio-Technica AT2020USBi Cardioid Condenser USB Microphone

This niche is great because there are endless customers for Microphones

Microphones are really cool, they are versatile and range from cheap to expensive and some even have built in karaoke functions.
Microphones are not cheap in the upper end of quality, but you can bet people will by them.

**Rock out in Profits with Electric Guitars**

- Fender Standard Telecaster Electric Guitar
- Squier by Fender Vintage Modified Jaguar Bass Special
- Epiphone Les Paul STANDARD Electric Guitar
- Squier by Fender "Stop Dreaming, Start Playing" Set
- Epiphone Les Paul Electric Guitar Player Package

This niche is great because there are endless customers for Guitars.
Electric guitars are a hot buy, yes; again they range from super cheap to real expensive so adjust accordingly.

Don't let expensive make you shy away from this niche, just check out one of the many reviews on Amazon to see how in demand they are.

**Tablets**

What would the niche money making on Amazon book be without mentioning Tablets, c'mon this is a niche I personally love, why? Because they make great gifts and they are always upgraded, even older models and versions sell well. Buyers are always flocking to this niche.

- Fire HD8
- Galaxy Tablet
- Kindle Voyage
- Amazon Echo
- Kindle Paper white 6"
- Samsung Galaxy Tab S3 9.7-Inch,
- Samsung Galaxy Tab A 8-Inch Tablet
- Samsung Galaxy View 18.4"; 32 GB Wifi Tablet
- Microsoft Surface 3 Tablet

This niche is great because there are endless customers for Tablets.
Face it, electronic items are always changing and upgrading fast, and this means more buyers for you.

Buyers are always there for this niche, because there trendy, are constantly being upgraded to newer versions and numbers.

**Cameras**

Okay, I know what you're thinking, why would anyone buy a camera nowadays with smart phones capability to take hot shots anytime anywhere. I'm here to tell you that cameras much like watches are here to stay, and you can make a lot of money with this niche. Don't listen to the naysayers.

- Canon EOS Rebel T6 Digital SLR Camera Kit with EF-S 18-55mm f/3.5-5.6 IS II Lens
- Nikon D3400 w/ AF-P DX NIKKOR 18-55mm f/3.5-5.6G VR
- Canon EOS Rebel T6 Digital SLR Camera Kit with EF-S 18-55mm and EF 75-300mm Zoom Lenses
- Nikon D3300 1532 18-55mm f/3.5-5.6G VR II Auto Focus-S DX NIKKOR Zoom Lens 24.2 MP Digital SLR
- Canon EOS Rebel T6i Digital SLR with EF-S 18-55mm IS STM Lens
- Panasonic LUMIX GH4 DMC-GH4GC-K 16.05MP Digital Single Lens Mirrorless Camera with 4K Cinematic Video
- Canon EF 24-70mm f/2.8L II USM Standard Zoom Lens

This niche is great because there are endless customers for Cameras.

People take pictures all day every day, from the old to the young.
There is a huge following when it comes to cameras, just step into any electronic store, or your local Costco and you'll see what I mean.

Cameras are not cheap, but there are buyers, I like this niche a lot.
No matter what anyone says, Smartphones will never take a timeless shot, sure you can snap a photo with ease with a Smartphone, but like a business card, cameras are here to stay.

**Smartphones**

- Apple iPhone 6 64GB 7-7+ X
- Apple iPhone 5S 16GB
- Samsung SM-G900V - Galaxy S5
- Samsung Galaxy J7 SM-J700H/DS
- Moto XT1644 G4 Plus (4th Gen)
- BLU VIVO XL2 - 5.5" 4G LTE

This niche is great because there are endless customers for smartphones.

Smartphones always have a following, they won't go anywhere, you can always count on a buyer..

Smartphone's always are being upgraded by the companies, so this leads to repeat sales for you.

The Smartphones niche has many opportunities to choose from don't be put off by what anyone says, you can make a lot of money.

**Headphones**

- Bose Quiet Comfort 35 Wireless Headphones
- Cowin E-7 Active Noise Cancelling Wireless Bluetooth Over-ear Stereo Headphones
- Bose QuietComfort 20 Acoustic Noise Cancelling Headphones
- Bose QuietComfort 25 Acoustic Noise Cancelling Headphones
- Sony Premium Noise Cancelling, Bluetooth Headphone
- Beats Studio Wireless Over-Ear Headphone

This niche is great because there are endless customers for headphones.

Headphones are very in demand, same as Smartphones they are trendy and always are being upgraded.

People love headphones, the buyer potential is very high, gyms, travel, you name it, there will always be buyers for this niche.

**Workout Watches**

- Samsung Gear S Smartwatch
- Huawei Watch
- Apple Watch Sport

This niche is great because there are endless customers for Workout Watches.

Smartwatches are very trendy and are always being upgraded.
People are very often willing to spend a lot of money in this niche since they're trying to keep trends and be flashy.

**Grooming products and sleep / fit monitors**

- Braun Series 9090cc Shaver
- Polar FT4 Heart Rate Monitor
- Fitbit Flex Sleep Monitor
- FitBit Smart Scale
- UP24 Jawbone
- Withings Smart Body Analyzer

This niche is great because there are endless customers for

This nice is awesome because many people are into keeping fit and healthy, and who doesn't love a great shave.
You can crossover to fitness niche and others with this.

**Bicycles, Tennis, Pool tables and more**

- Merax Finiss 26"
- Diamondback Bicycle
- RoyalBaby BMX Bike
- Bowflex PR1000 Home Gym
- Marcy Diamond Olympic Gy
- TRX Suspension Training
- Mizerak Billiard Table
- Joola Table Tennis
- Skywalker Trampoline

This niche is great because there are endless customers for Fitness Items.

Health is a huge profit niche, people will always spend money on health and fitness.

Gyms may come and go, but health products are here to stay.
Check out the endless reviews on Amazon if you are not convinced.

## Kitchen and Home Goods

- Amazon Fire TV
- Hyperikon LED
- Sensi Smart Thermostat
- Signature Sleep Contour Mattress
- Tuft & Needle Bed
- Stork Craft Hooper & Glider Ottoman Espresso Set
- Walker Edison 3 Peice Corner
- Office Star Air Chair
- Space Seating Chair

This niche is great because there are endless customers for Kitchen and Home Goods.

Many people want to make their homes look nice and beautiful whether in design or practicality, head over to IKEA and check out what's going on.

Mattresses and bedding items are a easy niche to get commissions off of whether you are promoting or earning.

## Garden, Patio and MORE

- Intex Spa
- AR Blue Clean Pressure Washer
- GreenWorks Amp Corded Snow Thrower
- Solar Panel Starter Kit
- Reliance Controls Portable Generator
- Fire Sense Commercial Patio Heater

This niche is great because there are endless customers for Garden and Patios.

People are always buying items for their garden and patio, the profits are endless.

The solar panels niche is very popular and quite expensive, no matter, all this means is potential for higher commissions.

**Pets Care Niche**

- Wireless Containment System
- 2 Speed Professional Animal Clipper
- Farm Innovators Model 4200 Pro Series
- Cosequin For Horses
- Purple Bravuara

This niche is great because there are endless customers for Pet Care.

Pet items are a hot commodity, and who doesn't love to take care of their pet. You can promote endless items with this niche.
One more reason, did I mention it already, people love their pets.

These are the Fantastic niches you will make the most profits from on Amazon. You can either be a promoter or an affiliate, or even dropship using Amazon FBA services.

Now how do we find items and products that are in high demand, in other words how do we make money?
Let's do it, I'll show you how. . . Then read on....

# HOW TO MAKE MONEY AND FIND EXPENSIVE, IN DEMAND PRODUCTS

For starters there is a There's a standard way and a FASTER WAY to find out and differentiate what are the most expensive items on Amazon, but not only this which ones are in high demand.

To do it the standard way go to **Amazon.com** use private mode (incognito mode) your browser of choice and search "department" that will take you to this page below:

For example; click on any area you have interest in as a niche, you should see a "best sellers" area, and then click on the best seller.

Look at the right side of the screen and you will see 'MORE TO EXPLORE' in the Department Name of choice, and directly below this you will see 'HOT NEW RELEASES,' 'MOVERS AND SHAKERS' and 'TOP RATED' .

Next, click to where it says 'See Top 100' within the 'Top Rated' category.

After clicking to see 'Top 100' Amazon will bring up the most highly rated products, these are usually the in "DEMAND" items.

Scroll through looking for many of the expensive products with a lot of reviews

As you can see this takes some time to do, while I still do this, there is a FASTER WAY to do it, as I showed earlier.

**NOW THE FASTER WAY....**

I I use the software called Ama Suite, This software is really neat because it streamlines your work, while it's not mandatory to purchase this to be successful. I didn't use any software in the beginning and I made a ton of money. Here are my earnings from my early days without software back

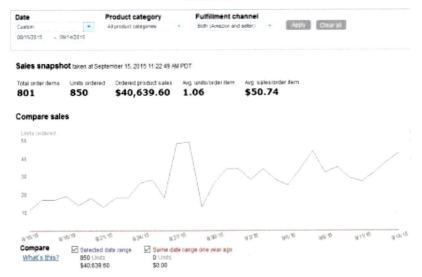

My earnings shot up substantially when I decided to purchase software. Again it is not mandatory.

Within Ama you can search for niche and differentiate from what products are making the most money, how much competition there is out there, meaning is the niche saturated or now. There are huge lists within Ama search capabilities which is linked to Amazons website, you enter a niche or criteria and priced at $200 and you will notice that 100 plus reviews will pop up in the software and will match many products to choose from.

Ama will show you data and keywords and that have low competition, which is excellent for what were after. You will have access to Google insight data and much much more. . .
Acess Ama at this link below:
**bit.ly/amaacct**

# HOW TO HACK YOUR WAY TO PROFITS

There are 3 options:

Create a review site to show off a product in high demand and rank the site.

Or create a price comparing website showing similar products and price ranges and reviews.

Create a blog or website to bold looking and professional, you can make the themes whatever you wish, even niche based, create a following. I use **BadNet,** they are the best in the business and walk you through every step of the way when creating a blog or website.
Acess Bad Net at the link Below:

**bit.ly/badnetcom**

**How to Create a Review Site**

Creating a review site is easy, you can base it off of any particular niche you like, the opportunity is endless. For example; you can review a niche product within fitness such as "treadmills" only and go from there, or E cigarettes, or any product and niche of your choice.

*Next Step is. . .*
To rank your newly created website in Google, and use terms such as "treadmills for home use reviews" or "e cigarettes reviews".

Now I'm not trying to promote Google as the number one in your money earning mission, remember Amazon is the bread winner here, the money maker. As you get more visitors to your site, these are all good, but focus on Amazon. Not to mention you would have to have strong SEO skills or

80

substantial amounts of money to set up different blogs and websites, which is just not feasible, but it's nice to know options.

Whether you have a site already, or use a ecommerce site, Amazon is the dominator. If you don't like this create your own website like Amazon, I am being serious, but that is a topic for another day, let's move on.

You should know who your competition is; there are multimillion dollar corporations that invest huge amounts of money into creating product review sites. They have teams, and disposable income. This is not to discourage you, but to get you acquainted with what's out there.

In short, it is hard to compete with Google due to their constantly updated algorithm.

# Conclusion

This is the best list of amazing products that are high priced and selling like crazy, you can feel free to search niches that suit your likes and tastes.

Many of these products have high commission rates and although the price tags vary from high to low, you will make money.

Take action now! The niche for profits is exploding and there is money in it for everybody, no matter how saturated the niches and products get. So whether you want to just get your feet wet for some extra cash, or need to pay off that loan, you can be worry free from now with the tools I have given you. Let's make money!!

Yours in Health and Wealth

Tim

And finally, if you liked the book, I would like to ask you to do me a favor and leave a review for the book on Amazon. Just go to your account on Amazon or click on the link below.

bit.ly/timsteinberg

Thank you and good luck!

# ABOUT THE AUTHOR

Tim Steinberg is a best-selling author and consultant for Fortune 500 companies, Exxon Mobil, Apple, Berkshire Hathaway, McKesson and Walmart.

Tim has been seen on the Joe Rogan Experience, 77 WABC Radio" "Where New York Comes To Talk," GQ Magazine, Muscle and Fitness Magazine, Playboy and more.

Tim has been able to go from being broke to making over $40,000 a month in record time; he now uses his time to help others to create the lifestyle they want, on their terms.

Many struggle with making ends meet and cash on hand just won't cut it and can seem daunting. Becoming rich and wealthy happens only when you have self determination and take action. Tim's books are step by step and easy to follow, the techniques laid out are simple, anyone can do it, stay at home mom's to the bustling entrepreneur, to the wealthy elite. No time, lots of time; doesn't matter with Tim's easy no holds barred methods. You will have the will and drive, along with money making techniques and special tips that will maximize your potential to rise to the ranks of rich status

Made in the USA
Lexington, KY
18 March 2018